ALSO BY GILI ESTLIN HIRSCH AND ALEX OGDEN:

Body of Work

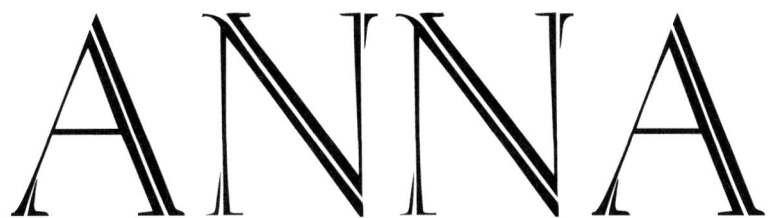

ANNA

Gili Estlin Hirsch

illustrated by Alex Ogden

FOX & OWL PRESS LLC ◆ SAINT PAUL, MN

Fox & Owl Press LLC may be contacted at foxandowlpress@gmail.com.

Published 2014 by Fox & Owl Press LLC
Cover design by Alex Ogden
Interior design by Alex Ogden
Printed in the United States of America

First Edition

ISBN 978-0-9892612-0-3

Fox & Owl Press
www.foxandowlpress.com

To Megan

Walk, Walk

ANNA

I AM SPEAKING TO YOU
From within a turned and muted breathing room,
Narrow at its tips like sand
At the beginning of its glorious glass journey,
But lush in its center stocked with quaking speaking corners
Woven of a sort of dusted residue
Of limelight.

Here, O Jerusalem,
He measures me
Not overly rhymed, if at all—
Sub
tle
Frills are unnecessary here, gratuitous,
Decorations.
Frowned upon.
You will not find here
The Psalms you were sung to as a child
Your sanctification will jut extrinsic filth all
Line breaks and jagged ink-in-ink
From the Hall of Praise within Your Kingdom, the
Small tapping noise at the sidewalk beneath
My home at the edge of an exhumed dawn

But know that I wanted to sing to you glory.

Jerusalem I am tied to you twice,
One by the word like the river Jordan,
One by the Poet like the gowns of the baptized

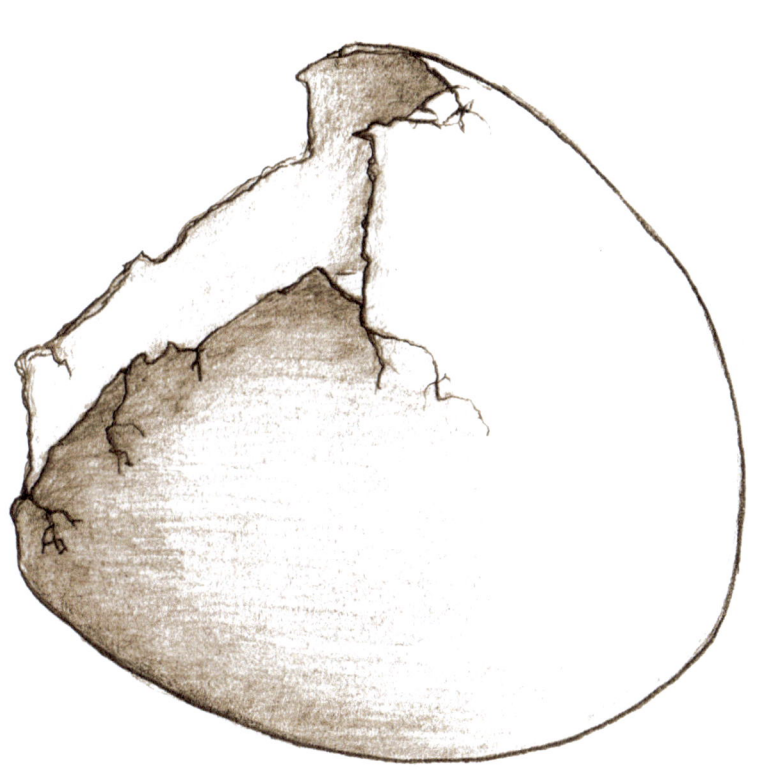

HALLEL/PRAISE

Praise
The receivers of seeds
Who never plant, but yearn
Who ache
Who spread and surrender;
Who mind with caution and care, who grow,
Who shield and water, who protect from storm,
Who strengthen with tears
And kneel with despair;
Praise the makers of peace
The bakers of bread
Who could not sanctify the ballots,
Could not vote with open palms at the Western Wall,
But were whipped at the plantations
And burned at the furnaces of Auschwitz
And deformed at Hiroshima
With a silent disloyal equality.

Praise our silent miraculous lovers
Lithe and rich in their moonlit dresses,
Soft and lush and moving,
Breathing and alive
Whose candy lips speak sweetly in our ears,
Whose eyelashes stroke our aching cheeks
Who breathe life within us
Who breathe life among us;

Praise our still and sighing mothers
Whose hands were hardened with the holy fire of stovetops
Who stood defiantly between us and raised arms and raised hills
And the downward slopes and the planes
Who breathed life within us
Who breathed life among us;
Praise our daughters
Whose great gentleness endures,
Coiling around itself like vines that stroke and penetrate
The deep and darkened places
In the hearts of ailing men;

Praise our widows
Our bereaved mothers
Praise the womb that buries soundlessly,
The only heart that gives to the earth its core and keeps on walking
above it,
Tending to tombstones with devotion,
Thumbing petals of flowers that rise
Over resting places of fallen sons.

Praise us
For we are submerged in the river Jordan
Enthroned in the golden domes and the white arches
Beset in the forests and in the forgotten lands;
We are pale and lovely in the sonnets
Wiley and crippling in the fairy tales
We are crude and seductive—we cross and uncross our long legs
In the red light of windows in Holland,
In the shadowy alleys of New York.

We are
Rachel and Leah and Sarah
We are Amelia and Golda
We are Sylvia, we are Virginia, we are Margaret,
We are all Mary
We are the sisters, the lovers
We are the mother of them all

The world with its trials sways and in its climax cries,
Collapses,

Praise us for we soothe it
We gather it unto ourselves
And rock it
Till it sleeps.

FIRST COMES LOVE

First Comes Love
And then the wind that carries the name
Over the newly created waters
And then comes the light
And from within it, the darkness,
And then come the stars.

The tree you and I are sitting in
Comes after love:
Comes after many roots and tangled reeds
And the sin of the desecrated soil,
The fall of the now-knowing
From the Garden of The Known.

I am compelled to warn you
As to the ropes
That lie on the other end of loving you
And I bow my head in saying,
My Love,
That our path's material is already made,
And we are merely stretching it at the ends
of it
Sewing the final cut and style
Of our already scaled fate;

But Love Comes First
The wind is silent now across the branches,
And the name serene
So let us kiss
And worry not of carriages
Or any such farce that comes before
Or after

THERE ARE GIRLS IN THESE TREES

There are girls in these trees; they are hiding
In the aching and burdening leaves.
The tree falls, summer falls, but they stay here and hover,
Holy and ready to grieve.

Humble and humble and close to the river,
They remain in their caskets unclaimed
With those who have walked and were nameless
And with those who were fallen and named.

Upon their return to their alleyway mornings
She emerged from their sights in the blood
No harp resounds her but leather untangling,
No holy water but mud

And they say that she chose me; I recall with confusion
The swift alteration of planes
In this winter, then, I am forgotten,
And her broken body remains.

(There is peace here, but over the fence,
The masses inevitably riot.
She told me, 'If I wanted silence,
I'd have stayed by myself and kept quiet.')

JERUSALEM 2010

At the horizon yesterday,
Jerusalem lit so violently with heat and with sweat,
That it seemed almost gleaming with snow.

I stood in its light;
The over-exposed white Mounts were weeping,
Spreading frantic, bald forests below.

When I walk at these Palestine floors,
Like a wind memory, I'm always stepping on hearts
That fell there with nothing to show;

And the coasts are removed from me, distant,
And I forget what I told you; a yes,
Or a crippling no

CONFESSIONAL

I listen to the shifts in your breath like hymns. You shake with a
murmur and the air rolls
off your back like a
sacred, sacred
and I connect in times like these. Words whirl into my head and from my
mind
to my quivering mouth on your shoulder and I whisper them swiftly
like a prayer made for the acerbic ceiling and the
cruel, misunderstanding walls
Bless The Temple On Your Sanctified Features
This is my hall of profession within your Jerusalem.

Dawn bites back against the night, arching—
etch my confessional in bleeding ink upon your skin lest you cease to
inhale down the
beat of my touch
by the curve of your spine.

MY MOTHER READ POEMS TO ME

My mother read poems to me,
Out loud,
When I was only
A young child:
There were specialists at that time that had said
That reading poems to babies
Would sharpen
Their later skills
In mathematics.
What was it then that
Rocked thousands of children to sleep
At the knees of Yeats and Whitman,
Neruda and
Frost?
The seesaw lullaby iambic makes,
Back and forth, like a
Lunatic equation with its
Unadulterated ticking? Or was it
The drawer-bent free verse
Of some
Chained-to-white scientist?

My mother read poems to me,
Out loud,
When I was only
A young child,
Because she wanted me
To be good at maths;
I feel bad for my mother for
Many reasons: one of them
Is that I despise arithmetic.
All of the careful meter
That she spoke at me
Served only to make me
A confounded lover of words,
Weak in the knees at the whispered
Wished women of a young Cohen,
Bent at the waist and spread open with only a
D-d-drip of cummings'

r-p-o-p-h-e-s-s-a-g-r

I think sometimes, let us appease good Jewish
mothers:
Why not crash this poet's bones
At the spinning helm
And burn her by the coast.
From her ashes a mathematician may appear,
Like a phoenix.

NIGHTINGALE

My Nightingale,
My frozen limbs untangle with your whispered spell.
The arching heights of me stand to draw watercolor skies
When you ring the ancient sunrise's early bell.

They used to tell a tale
Under bowed clouds in the veil
Of the nighttime's rich intoxicating seep,
That all the women-birds said, let us sleep;
And in the morning, we'll regale.
But you stood upon the steamy cooling hail
Where the earth was bound to leap
And you sang,
Though you were frail,
And earth was steep;
You sang, and it was liquid heat run deep
Into the core of every instance like a weep,
And like a dove within a jail
My heart was honey in the pale.

When you come upon the branches of my keep,
My battered stem can finally exhale.

ALTARS RISE AMISS

Altars rise amiss
At the arch of my back
At the heel of sister Palestine:
In an aberrant chronology,
Sick like thunder rolling
Ahead of the spark in the sky,
I carve out intake first—
foodairwarmth—
Then fan the outflow,
words words words.

Cut

Short

From the intrinsic tilt,
I break my fall face first.
The lightning came last,
The day has been victorious over me,
I lament no one.

I LEFT ALL MY HYMNS

I left all my hymns to the breadth of the shadows
To the things that are floral and sleek
But my voice warped and broke on her hinges
Where I turned and intended to speak
And my chest went and sought her in bones
To tourniquet where she had leaked

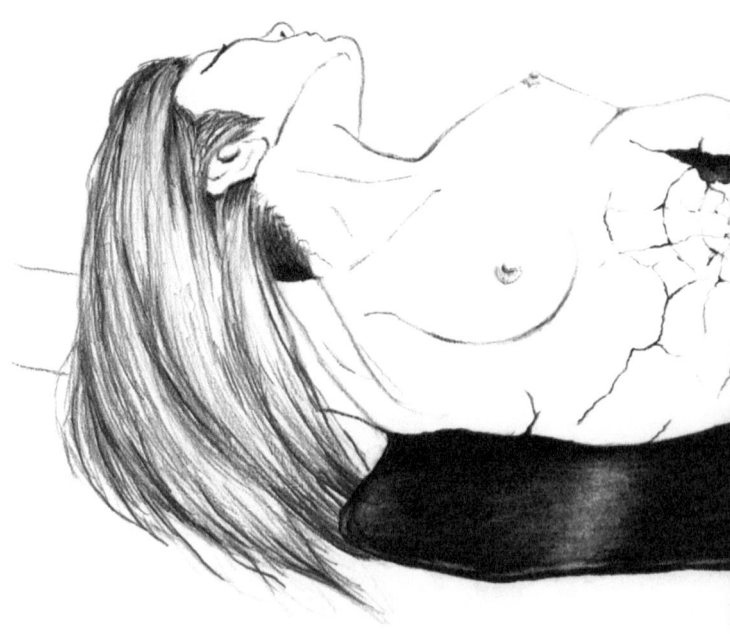

But found only a quivering outline,
And became very timid and meek
So my ruptured tongue lies with her brethren
In a grave that is strange and opaque,
But she wakes in the nighttimes to haunt me
In the very few places I seek.

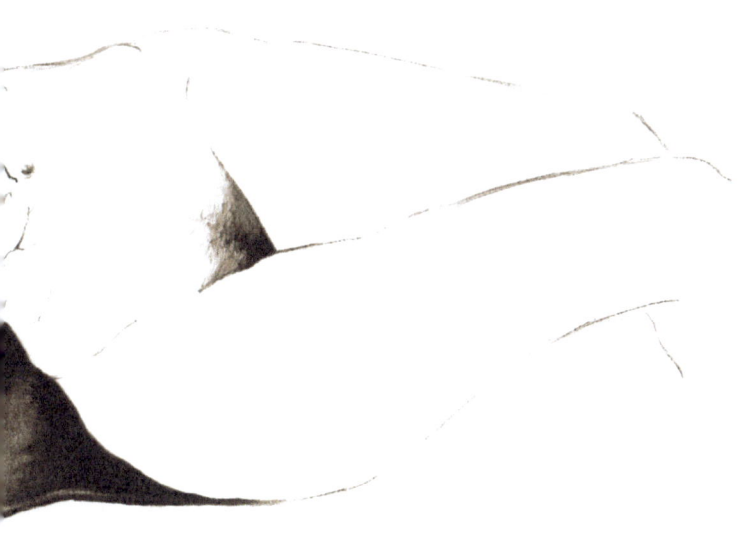

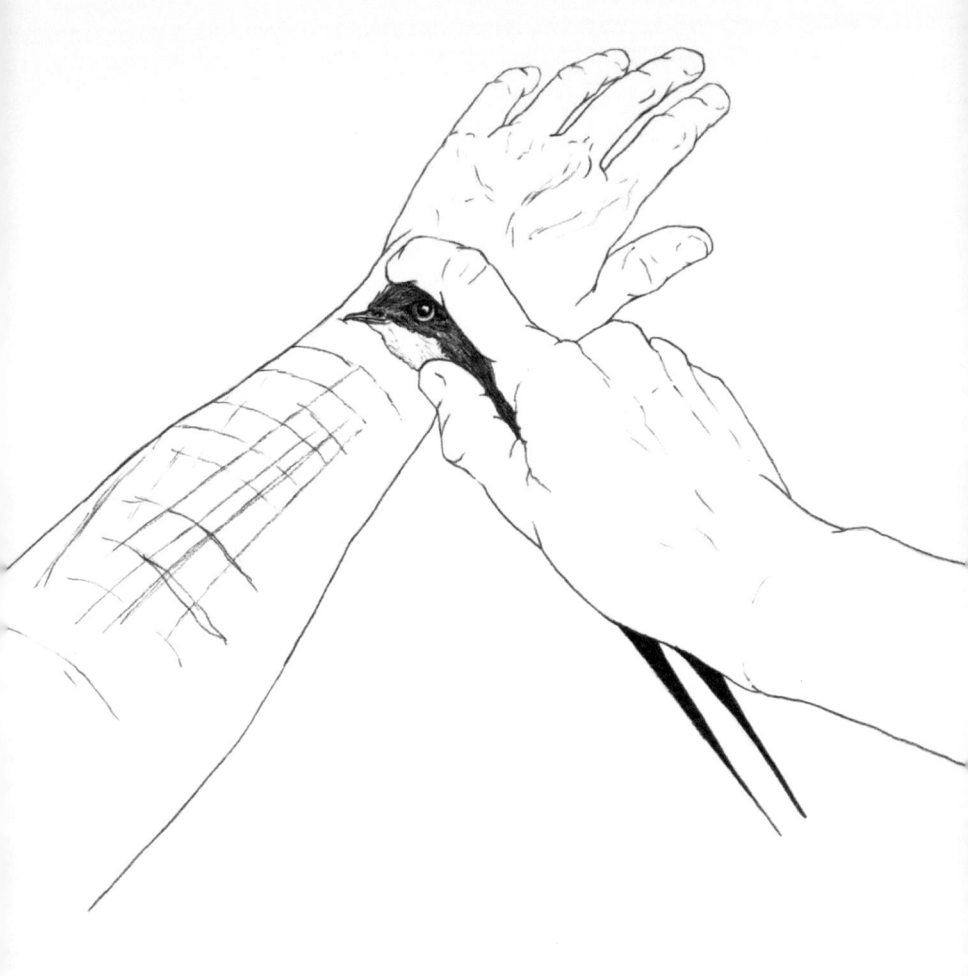

CRUXIFICTION #6

Under casketed archways and in rooms with no sun
My legs will falter, darling, my mouth will dry of rhyme;
The night has whispered you to me at least a million times;
Another nail in place, my body comes undone,

A cross is for the fiction—it holds no hidden treasure
I cannot keep my tongue from speaking out your name;
When metal hits the skin, the wish is hard to tame;
Pray another lullaby in silence for good measure

They lift the wood together; the shadows on the ground
Resemble mathematics (when they were slightly older)
A ragged piece of flesh is torn across my shoulder
The faith lays there forgotten, the press of passion found

At the base of your thighs, as the moisture there proves
The rain falls on the dead, and on the living who are still;
The rust that curses through my veins will not undo the will;
In all of the layers, something still moves.

FOR IPEK

silk;
what is it you reared in me so fearlessly
dumbstruck on the corner
of massachusetts ave?
honeyed and soft, you
were yielding
your storyteller eyes
pierced through my fibbing heart.
come back to me rhythm rhythm
come back to me you are the virtue
of the miraculous lines, you compose
it with your fingertips.

you grow in me like a child
not in the space that empties and bleeds
but in the hushed speaking place
under my heart
over my spleen
at the tip
of my breath
less
lungs

you can be woven
into luscious robes
pierce-marked with
unspeakable prices

but i like you best
wild
crawling with the babies
that made you,
shining with the prism
innate in your skin

INK

raleigh like
north Carolina, two
hours west
 of atlantic beach
tell
 'em
how we sparked
 at our edges all
midnight electric,
 blunt
candescent
 force igniting
 at the
pit of our
stomachs
   hitting
   stone
   hitting
stone again and again
 till we
  lit and stained
scissor marked fire
   all over the sheets

i want
  to
spread
  for you
 like
Ink
 at the heel
of the
 press

city of
  oaks you are
pooling at my thighs like
  the cock of a gun,
sudden-and-
thick-
    pouring
  at the base of
  me
like
 the rush that
hisses in
 a blind man's
ear
 after the

  click

WIRED NOTIONS, MID AIR

YOU are an epic—
The famed journey down to San Francisco.
There is an air of sweetness and smoke
At the edges of your voice,
Like Ophelia's cries of distress
Around her contentment.
You are rejoicing and worshiping
At the foot of Mount Sinai
Against the decree and the commandment,
But with the spirit,
And with the might of a thousand lifetimes
To praise.

My father bounded great heights;
My grandfather was a man of the sea.
I used to be at ease only at plains
But my genetics stirred at me
And I began
Jumping very high
And diving very deep.

Your hands unwound great secrets
Beneath the six-pointed shield,
Unearthed me where I was struck
Beneath layers of the ashes that remain
From poetry and ache;
I fashioned myself a shield made of history
And other such injuries
It disassembled itself, however, and,
Though I had tried to retrieve it,
Remained with the grains I shook from my eyelashes
When you found me.

And so
We live in an artist's vice.
Today I shall ring out my masterpiece.

WHY WE RISE

What is it
That wakes you in the daytime
And stirs you to say:
"I must"?
Do you not know
Your arms are too short
To box with God?

CAVITY

Everything I write I write to you now,
And everything I sing I sing to you,
And the untold roads are our own roads
Upon the falls
And at the filling places of the press and of the pen.
Everything I write, I write to you now,
Since the dark room where my back curved
Under your hand, my legs
Pushing into framed canvases of scholarly attempts,
And your hair brushed my neck
And I caked at your fingers and around your palm,
And I said for the first time, "Don't Stop"
And for the very first time, you said,
"Never".
I saw there already the encrypted wound lace and
The etching, how abysmal stardust
Will sprinkle our footpath and thicken our pace.
Almost to a halt but still we walk—
Just about—
A saccharine tip of a rust riddled end, these
Minute-waltz sways between
The one and two,
Between the
Cut and mend.

We're only just children, love; how do we know
Where the carving knives go
And the angles to draw the most blood?
Your heart is the brick to my archways,
Your bite is the dam to my flood.

DON'T CALL AT ME

Don't call at me as if you have
Some kind of pull
With luminary luck.
whatever pain the earth leaves at her turning
pounds at me
until my barely mended knee bucks;
i'm spread wide on her kitchen counter,
such a goddamn whore
for planetary fucks

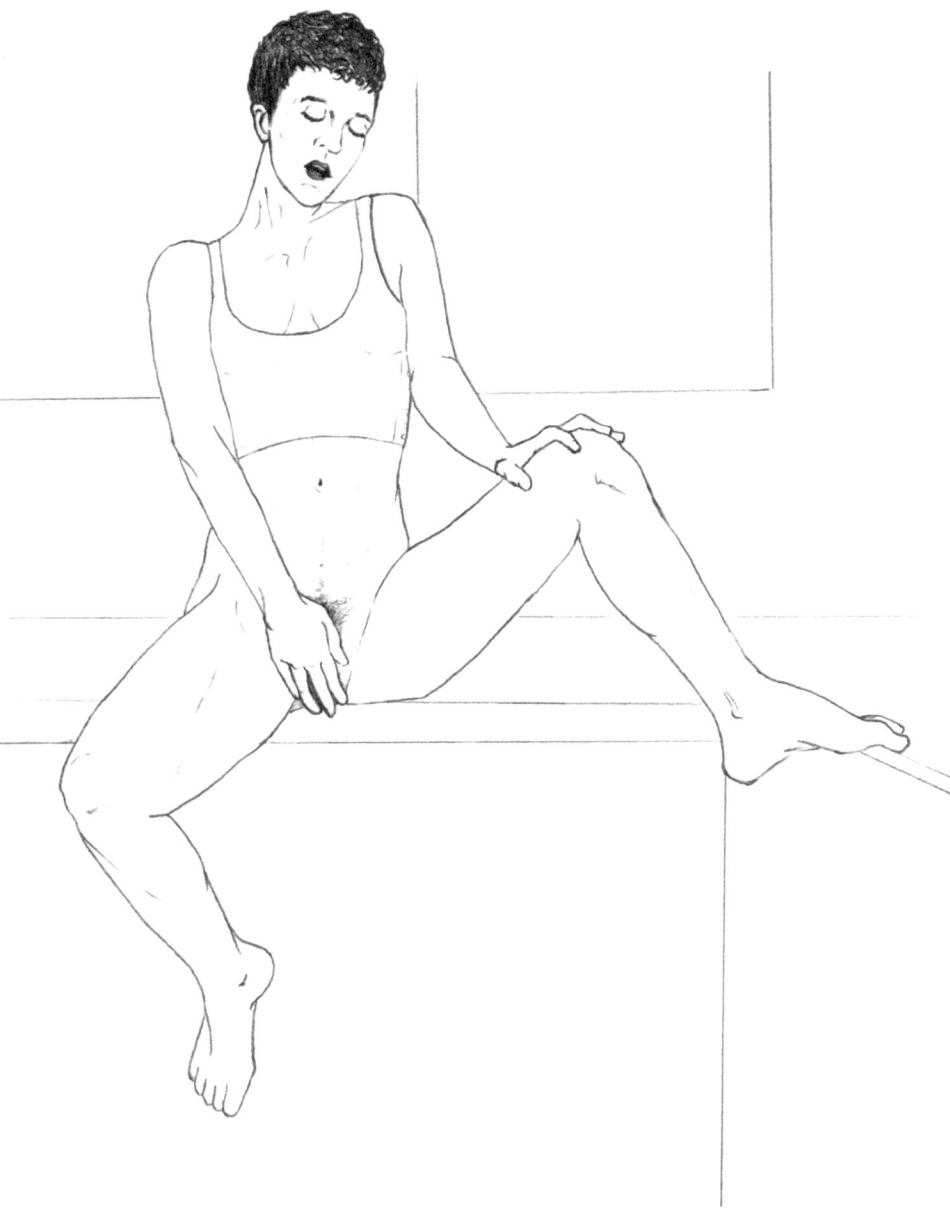

MEET ME WHERE MY SKIN HAS SPLIT

Meet me where my skin has split
Of both of us, I'm at fault of it,
But I held her vein to the blade, as well,
Our bodies sway with the ringing bell.

Good intent won't save from greed—
A quick incision's all one needs,
Although it must be deep with hope;
Our bodies swing from the ringing rope.

IF YOU LEAVE (DUET)

(I will beat like hidden treasures do
Beneath the solid rock:
They'll have to dig for me, my love, long having
Sketched me with their chalk.)

What of this shell, then, and what of the beat—
Our rocking's bent.
I dug you from the dirt each night
I sketched you naked in our tent.

(Then I will fall, and all my floral hush
Will fall along as well.
I'll cock the gun. I'll fasten nooses
On the rope that rings the bell.)

I've brought you hushed and hushing flowers
In the fall and in the spring.
If by your fastened force or by its own, my love,
The bell will ring.

(My lifted palms will cradle nails, then, in the wood,
My ivory skinned,
And not a minyan that you dare to raise
Could lift me to the wind.)

So I will press my palms in prayer
To every Ivory idol thus;
The day will rise and raise, my love.
The wind itself will carry us.

The night that ushers you ahead
Will nip your ankles in the end
And brush your hair and break your bread
Until your cross will die and bend.

(This cloak that you've devised
And rested on my head,
Is shivering at the graveyard
Beside your mother's bed.)

NO MATTER WHAT

He told me once that I could
Put half a Klonopin under my tongue
And go to sleep—
No matter what,
and that night up north
We wound it up with dollar bills
And felt very celebratory.
It hurt
Going through my system
Going through my nostrils,
and he hurt
Swallowing down my throat, like a
Pill that is too big.
I don't play, I just know
What to fuck around with and
what not to fuck around with
And if that makes me smart,
Then fine, and if
That makes you a fool for the
Drip and the hospital bed
That's fine too.

A killer at my thighs
You left cigarette burns
All over the inside of my stomach
And now I throw up blood
Whenever you cross my chest—
No matter what.

BE GENTLE WITH THESE CUTS

be gentle with these cuts—

what defiant wishes, these cuts were not
born from gentleness or within it; you saw
the motion of the razor-bow over the strings of my skin,
how the canvas shook, instruments like these
take years to master
you are a printmaker, surely you know how
precious the course is, how thick and kind the brutal
press, I wouldn't come into your gallery and dilute
swiftness upon your fabrics
I respect the path of them, the ink-oil-plate-knife-paper of them,
I respect
the steady-steady-slow and over-and-over of them, I know that
it is holy, I don't
cast at them with sudden changes of heart and color or
shapes that are not premeditated. so you can't pour
tenderness and sanitation over me—I birthed these
visceral and harsh, carved them ruthless, do not
clean this,
the rush-hurried-vicious of it,
the fury-wrath sharpness of it,
seal these and I'll have to make new ones
and I am running
out of room

CONFUSED? ALLOW ME TO ILLUMINATE

IF a string is burning at both its ends then
I am a 16-ply medium coiled tight engulfed in wildfires
From within and without. There are
Different kinds of blood here: the heavy
Lumpy brown-and-purple bathwater blood I
Dumped her out with
(Unintentionally), the blood from last month's
Broken teeth pink, caked all over the swell of my
Heartbeat and my spread
Thighs, the scissor-marked finger drawn blood
You left here on the sheets last week, a
Strange thin mud color diluted into cotton,
And then there is this blood, my blood,
I beckon it like the west wind
Calls forth at the east, writing at it, coaxing
At its walls to warp and
Give in. Like I did at yours.

Remember?

The knife cuts the string,
The fire
Abates;

Consider it a venous extinguisher fluid,
Thick and rich and red like
Good, old wine
At the burn.

        (If I had slept in your bed last night I would have
        Left an impress made of blood like the
        Stripes of a tiger; maybe then you would have
        Better understood, but unfortunately,
        I slept elsewhere)

THEY RETURNED ME TO THE POND

They returned me to the pond. We've heard of girls like you before; the heavenly unwind; have faith in us, the mute, the blind.

My maker in his wisdom, in your wisdom's breath untold. I've been cleansed on the riverbank, a precious find; come beg to me, the sick, the kind.

I knew you on the turning. The wolves lurk in the winter, the casket lays uncovered, my mother's ghost had hovered; past the fence, I lost my mind.

I told them how I weaved my hands together, and laid them on my chest; I told Jesus, then, to come. The shadows make a print of something strange; the water lilies hum.

We stood in pairs together in the middle of the yard, and the flash was blinding. They call those girls in skirts a waste—that one unending chase was chaste.

I whispered to the pines my wish in red and white, breaking on the morning's end: the days still seem to bend. I walk alone. My steps are light.

RIVIERA MENTAL

1.

We'll open with the state of arts,
And now, on to the play:
He was very kind
But lonesome on his way.
She was charming, iridescent,
With lightning coals for hair,
And ivory for skin
And schizophrenia for prayer.
And her smile was so brilliant
And lit so many corners
That it made dancers out of cripples
And believers out of mourners,
And when they met upon the break
Of ordinary days
How could either of them know
The going of the ways.

2.

It's so hard to make friends with you, Charles.
The man I only heard of broke my heart and now it is
Frayed
Like pieces of a broken mirror, scattered on the ground
And reflecting the remnants of the sun
At twilight.
I told you already, I do not want a drink
I don't want a cold compress, either, my head hurts because
It works too hard, too much, not because I'm sick
Or anything like that.
Charles, stop pacing
You'll bruise the floor or your feet
It's not worth it.
You cannot fix me any better than I can fix myself
These waters will drown and surround us
And will be victorious
In the end.

3.

I rested on an ancient girl
I hardly knew her
Before I crossed and swore my heart
That I'd be truer
I gave her everything I had
I didn't mind
That she was utterly unmade
The broken kind
The night had took her mind complete
Riviera Mental
I followed her there, to the dark
The wild the gentle
She swayed and then she fell and ruined
Her biggest fan
I swam in after, now I am
Her dented man

4.

Charles, I apologize for this.
Perhaps our biggest victory is not yet in our midst.
Surely you know that this is not what I had wanted
For you
I did not even want this for me
But I am at peace now, complete
And better. I am yours only in halves
And the cracks in between belong
To the rivers that wait, that creep upon my feet
That beg of me
To walk amongst them.
They are stronger than you, so please,
Stop trying to defeat their current.
It is my lifetime, Charles, and upon my lifetime,
I exist
Only in the space
Between the tides.

YOU DIDN'T WANT TO END LIKE THIS

You didn't want to end like this,
But this is how it ends—
No more than keeled internals on the day's sweet bend,
Like the waves from her strings and your ink's tight blend
On the copper, in the gates, Godspeed, heaven send.
This is how I kill you: from my bed across the land,
Not sweet pearls like I promised,
Only tar-stained sand
An unhinging like a swing,
Rock the turf and fuck the band,
No foreign fingers round your neck

It's just my hand

It's just my hand.

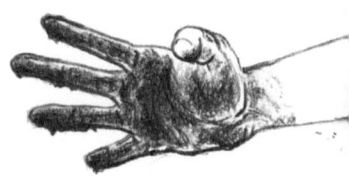

LETTER TO BOSTON

City, remember when I came to you unwound, undiluted, unmade, and you embraced me so wildly with your wayward raindrops? On the bridge where she and I held hands, at the key of the undying old tin door, home, you—swallow me whole. You bid me a silence that I cannot regret. In the lowered places where the moisture lay for me to taste; you spun all round us at an equal pace, so ready to frame this love affair, so dismantled always moving lovely, lovely, gentle in your hills, but vicious in the underscore, just like we were: you walked with us. And I thank you for it. You walked with us like a loyal dog where we came together in short lived explosions, cataclysms of joy, you—turned your face from the frozen rivers where we made love and let your spirits lash at our hairs, at her hair that was still long then and lush, that was still mine, and you spared us your brush strokes and freed us of judgment, praise, you made a haven for our terrestrial fucks and the linear weaving of our hands. And then when it cracked you rested your elfish head at our laps innocently and knocked us together again and again. And our knees became rusted from knocking, from trying desperately to crawl forward; from falling on them and praying with the great spirits and howling to your four-directional-wind to please not let it end, please, please, please, don't keep it from us, and your whirlwind carried all-of-it-or-nothing to the Gods. She and I came down like your heavy snow on Harvard Yard, thick and insistent, trying against hope to cover something old that has been walked on with some heaven made linen, except yours was water, and ours was love.

Oh, blessed paved paths of illusion. City, you maintained the backdrop seamlessly when the seaming was all we had. In the beating center of you, under the soft curve of dawn, my hand at the small of her back was sealed in your minutes like handprints in soft wet cement. And I know that you remember the bow of our heads where your days met your evenings, in the roads and in the lakes and in the bed, and in the space between our fingers that we could not narrow well enough, the crack you always managed to bust and swim through, pour out, stain us.

Don't be—coy. You're a part of this. As much a part of this as we were. And yes, we danced, and yes, we were tied to the corners of the great speaking things and you held us still in spaces that can be measured with a beating of a drum. Or of a heart. Did we not press foreheads together and swear to forever when your seasons dropped changing like a guillotine blade, no soft shifting, no warning before the strangling sensation of heat fell over us like the end of notes? And did we not walk even in the heat and suffocation, the sweat gathering at the base of our clavicles and dripping to your core as we moved and moved, all lovely and new-built dismantled we moved?

Now I see your streets are soaring slowly, plotting to push us together, like the tilting of a plaything when it lies idly in some playing hand. The tiny metal spheres, she and I, the cheap plastic neon frame you and your wicked inertia. Hush, you'll speak to us like a mother at nighttime, hush, you'll tuck us in under separate beds between different walls, shaken walls. So close—your smoggy air is slipping densely through my nostrils and hers and then through her perfect mouth at my hip in my mind and then through my mouth. From my vine-pressed corner I am pressing my legs together once more, press us in you together once more, so that my lungs can fill with little fluttering dying birds begging to rest from their endless seizing, from our tiring journey.

Will she buck, my cosmic love? Can you hear my cosmic prayer when I pace in your streets, to bring us back to your riverbed and strike there our final match, and be consumed, or not consumed, but just to be—till the morning sun, while the dust of it still settles in my deafened body, to wake me with your rain and her hand at the base of my thighs, as if all of it has been nothing but a bad city dream, and all we'd have to do is escape your low skyline and we'd be fine?

ALAS

who knows where the carving knives go?
where the storybooks run when they whisper and glow?
how I carried you far to our home, on the street,
and your legs wrapped around me, the sweet
breath of vodka and praise to the lord on your breath
on your tongue
on my breath
in my lungs
we were two
we were one
we were two
you were young
when the hilt of our slope disappeared and amassed
now I know where the storybooks go, and
the carving knives
even more so.

Alas.

SEVEN FOR ANNE

I'm splitting at the places that you
Taught me not to show;
It's more a tube-fed kind of inward shove
Of knowledge than a hunch, to still remember how
Even little schoolboys know
There's no such beast as
Everlasting love.

AXIS

Corners cut in stone, I
fight, shedding darkness over
light;
sunrise length and sunrise
height, sunset mornings, sunset
nights.

We were tigers, you and I, and thus our roar's our
lullaby;
what has been made we can't
untie. At night, alone, we race the
sky.

I marry beds, divorce
cement. They say I measure what He
meant,
proclaiming how it's heaven
sent: it's just the way the fortunes
went.

Our words would sway from side to
side. I remember when you
died;
the band director waved and
smiled, the coffin hissed, the crowd went
wild.
The tempo low, the beat got
higher, the melody a (lenient)
liar.
We dip our feet in fields of
mire and holy fire, broken
fire.

This harmony, so ill and
aided, reminded me of how we
dated,
Homebound, and serenely fated.

Slow and painful.

(But we made it.)

CHILDREN WHO WERE BORN

Children who were born after this all started
Never saw birds before,
It occurred to me.
If they should ever return here—
The birds or the children—
They will stare at one another oddly
And with great consideration
Their respective colors shining, amplified
Against the dusty backdrop
Of this revolution
And instead of hitting feathers or skin with the edges of guns
They will be so shocked
That they will stand still across from one another with open mouths
And say nothing.

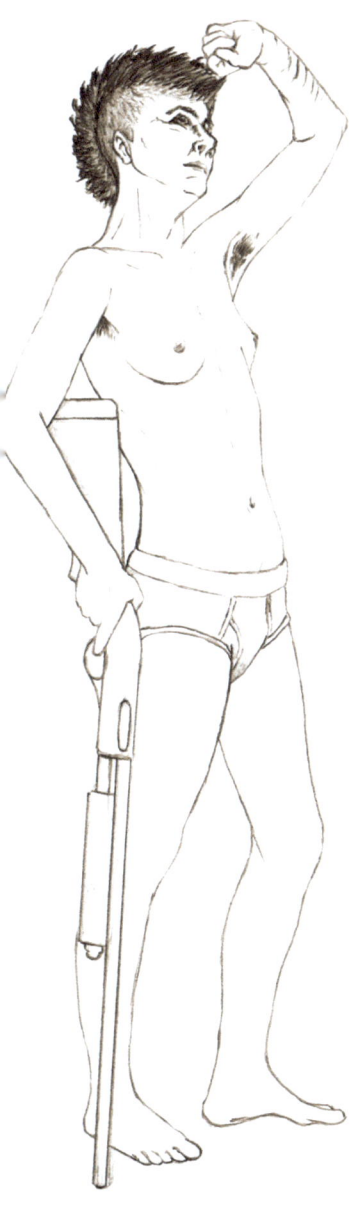

SCHULTZ

there is a small silken graveyard pressed
between my ribs, and sounding there is
a muted hush of all the breaths of the walking-things we tried to save
he and i
and kept in boxes in his room, contracting
all manners of diseases;
and more loudly all those we could not save
and never knew to try.
you stir there quietly sometimes among them,
flush against my spine
flinching from the lines in the path even in your sleep,
so afraid there is a curse there,
in the space between one tile
and the next.

PORTSMOUTH LAMENT

I'd howl for you each evening at the pier
At Prescott Park with a sugar high
An opium dagger at my throat
A knot I don't know to untie
I can't return, I told you why
The rowing boats and I
will wait for you each night

My misery and I
We made a pact to try
And carry on without you, even if
The very thought
Unhinged and stopped the world with a sigh
That you could hear still in your bed
A few blocks down the road
A killed goodbye
It danced about, it laced your precious ears
With love and lust and lies

I cannot stop you now, I couldn't stop you then—
You chose to fly
The words you breathe will always mark my sun
And baptize every sky,
And every sunrise, every summit
Will always wrap me with your voice, and I will cry
Forever at the top of every hill
That it should have been the two of us, not you
And not just I, that if it had to end
I wish I'd ended too, all slick and sly
Instead of learning how to be without you
Halved and hollowed dry

We were like waves and shores and so, therefore
It is our destiny to vie for kisses that can never be
A broken bird that cannot fly
We'd put it down to sleep, and just more flesh revealed
In my indefinite supply
I won't forget you, you're like roses in the rain
In mid–July, and we'll go by
And time will mend and heal, but I will always
Howl for you with every sugar rush and every
Passing midnight eye
And that will be our lot
To love and lose is best, you chose to fly
You said yourself—you were my air
and every breath we took was knives
Alas, my love
You will remain
The very hinges of my thigh
Whenever more I choose to dance
And bend for you
You chose to fly.

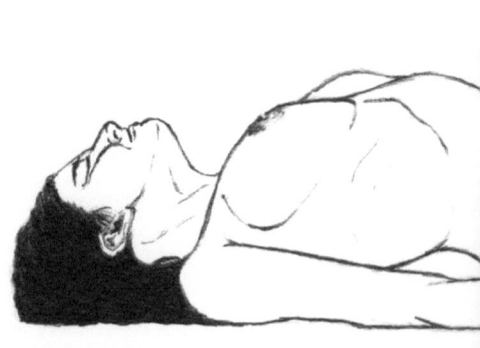

BYOB I

we're only hours away from
greatness
just strip naked now before
this untold path and lift your
palms and scream the headiest scream
you can come up with and
someone's god will hear you already,
fall to your knees and demand a revelation,
a revolution, a riot, demand
some sweet justice at the heel
of the mount at the heel of your foot,

at—

the—

heel—

of—

the—

press—

dunk your head beneath the icy river, slide
wrist deep into some tight pussy, ask him
to tie your hands behind your back and pound at
you
until all the wound
yarned
laced post-traumatic-post
  –modernistic–prehistoric–
rage–stress is humiliated defeated struck and
curls itself roaming inside you silenced gagged
and slaps itself to sleep at the apex of your
ribcage like some bitch i knew who liked it rough,

oh god being far from you is a life
sentence at hard labor, god you're
good at keeping silent, god if i squeeze at you
hard enough will all the words
come pouring out and drip
at my fingers like
baby spiders or pus or honey or
god you fight a good solid fight, who taught
you how to fight like this, who taught you
how to coax drop hiss someone like that to
their knees with a bitten tiding
tongue, don't you
know that is goddamn disrespectful?
god i want you between my thighs already
i'll make you a trade:
ink for words,
step for
step

BYOB II

Don't ask me questions I cannot
Answer for you. What lost teeth? Maybe
When we boxed that one
Time. You know, I didn't
Even taste that blood. The wedding bells the knockout bell,
It gunned me all
the same.

Let me take you to the falls.
Don't be grinding teeth like that
In these deafening leaves of grass
If you want to hunt;
You are giving up your site.
And I can see you anyway.
Your stride here doesn't
Fool me. Don't clench your
Fists so hard. Even that hard fist was
Once an open palm with
Fingers, and they
Fit so perfectly inside of me if only you
Could open I could
Open.

Speak to me then with your animal tongue,
Lap at me then
With your animal
Tongue. I want your hollows and your sacred
Saunter kick-kick-kicking at my
Overly
Soft
—ness

Let me take you to the falls.
You'll be the lioness and I'll be the foal.
You will be Midas and I'll be your wife.
And who is the lamb here?
And who is the knife?

BYOB III

I will pen you all the poems that scrolls can band;
From your fingers to your thighs, to the
Cliff at which you stand—Ink
On every millimeter of your skin, meter to drown out the
draining sink.
That someone had broke into you
When your shell was very thin.
Without permission. To sing loudly over
Any unseen stitches at the roof of your sweet mouth,
At the muscles of your shins.

I'll write you words, but will words find and rock you?
My words? Or at all?
Will the swell of sweet iambic rush through the veins
Of your cracked and crooked wall? Medicinal,
Unbent, will it weigh this seesaw down so that you
Slide my way? (Or fall?)

Whenever you are near me, I memorize
The creases at your brow and at your core.
I never know if you'll return
like dust to dust, or like a lover
From the war. Or like wind chimes in a wind I cannot feel,
Or like a print hung in a house that has no door.
So I remember you while, at, when you are inside me.
Abysmal sand in constant ache
For winter waves that briefly were the shore.

BRUISES OR BLISS

I cut at my chest and handed my heart all throbbing—
He still didn't know to dismiss it.
I bucked at my knee and he bent down to kiss it.
How will I know if I hit it or miss it?

Words that are spoken invite their own burden
How would you know that, if you died a virgin?
How would you know that at the end of the ocean
They know only one prayer, the lips' quickened motion,

The arch of the back, and the tongue's sudden hissing.
Not a gift that you're poured with just upon being christened.
Won't you come back to us, father, in bits and a piece
For all we know, we'd learned from your tyrants and you
How to build homes and countries, and an enemy's cease
Like the sunrise uprising on a victorious view.
She will not hide—
She will gently kiss your hand, if you were to give it
In her teeth the ships attack upon another's request
And the dark used to bide
And yet now it is bit.
She can't even sleep now
And wears war-paint for make-up
The slice of the breakup
Is drilling her neck.

We all know we lack
A thing in the wind
That was never taught.
In the end, though
We seem to wrap ourselves about it
With the lot

I said all my prayers, but the sky is remiss;
Still he will pray for the virginal you.
Alas, the abyss; there is this and there's this.
How will we know if we're bruises or bliss?

WILHELM TELL

Let's play Wilhelm Tell like Burroughs and Joan
With the crook of your finger
And my heartbroken moan.
Come home to Ithaca, covered in shields;
I am Penelope if you roam in the fields.
The cut and the length of your press is upon us,
The hitch of the breath and the nape of the tell—
That you also remember the arch and the swell.
I will wait for the fold with the spark and a groan.

Marry King Mark, then, if you fear it—
And have a fate lost to the height.
I will still remain Tristan,
And you'll call out to me every night.

WHAT LEONARD WROTE

Former lover speak to me, I am
Trying to prove Mori wrong.
For all the star-filled nights that he spent with Roshi in San Gabriel
He must know a thing or two
About love,
But when you slid your precious fingers into me, and
The crystalline jive of white noise pressed its heavy heel to our window
And the dull thrust of streetwise motion
Hummed in time with the rush at
Your bitten pulse point, were we really only retracing
A line in the ancient sand that someone else had
Made with sweat and tears and love and come? Former lover,
I won't believe it
Although I know it is vicious
To question your teacher.
The decision-makers up at Mt. Baldy would have us think
That our bounding rhythm was only some past-life-compounded
Tread of the mind, evolution and chemistry when
Your cheekbone dug at the flesh of my thigh,
Neurons lover and not magic
Where your tongue rested against me so soft so—silver breathless soft
That I wanted to fold myself over a million times, that I could
Have just
Died.

Lover, lover, no,
I know from where you rest against my ribs
And where I ache you at the tip of my lungs
That no one knew us before us, and that the castles we built
With our woven hands were made of new grains and new
Water from oceans that no one
Had breathed in.
Oh, speak to me my lover, my midnight hush, I am
Without rivers in the dark without you
Speak to me; I am so lost and raw
Without your strings.

When I walk upon this city, I still pray in verse
To the beat of strange men's steps
That you will sing to me yet in lazy mornings
What Leonard Wrote
About forests and lovers
And then whisper in my ear that he always was
Wrong
When it came to you and me.

FOR L.N.C.

Break a bottle of liquor upon my chest, bless
Me like a newly launched ship. Dip
My hips in something wild: Child,
I've told you that one, now, how
The days will be unkind, mind
The swift exoneration, nations
Will fall down at your feet, meet
Them on the turning of the nights
Until the falling of the lights,
Until the days turn sweet.

I am a wretched ghost
I marry all my foes
She's shaking, boys, she's shaking,
But she's standing on her toes

*

in all this sacred mess,
in all this bitter suite,
whispering your name is holy matrimony
in the tour and out the tour and in the ceremony
i'll rush my blood for less
and spit out all my teeth.
i love you on the train
i love you on the edges
instead of only i and me i turn into The Virgin
the untold heart already cleanly cut out by the surgeon
i love you in the rain,
and in front of all the ledges.

The pictures hang outside without a frame.
I'd die without a whisper to my name.

PETRICHOR

Forgive me;
I think I was cruel to you
In the confusion
Of your boats
Rowing to shore
Without me,
In the press of my pen
I was cruel.
Forgive me:
I was born no fool,
But the dashing of objects
In the light and the darkness
Colored my view,
I left on that shore
What I trust to be true
And with ink and with heels
I was cruel.

Forgive me:
I was born no son
But the meet
Was real
At the core.

I am sorry
I altered
The score.

CATCH CALLS THE ONCE-LER

I speak for the trees for the trees have no tongues, I
Speak to the wind when I whisper your name, I
Have scarcely tongues enough to breathe it
Past my quivering lips from my quivering lungs
With its quivering nest of baby birds somewhat living somewhat
Dead and so frightened there with their mouth agape keening
For a warm touch and substance,
For a warm utterance
Or a motion of passion
They wish for it so badly and I wish so badly for them
To be hush-stricken and rooted in their place with love
Like I thought we were
But then I think—
They will only grow bigger and expand
And will try to fly only to be broken at tepid winds,
No room there to take height
That they will be heartbroken on the ground
Or dead at flight.

And I feel for them, so in their sleep
Sometimes I push a bit
On the feathered surface of their throat.
And they die a bit each night.

I LOVE YOU, YOU ARE VERY

I love you, you are very
soft around your edges, I love you;
The slope of your altering nose
buried in my thigh is upon me when I say grace
at dinnertime and pray for the abundance, my time tied tongue
lapping at the milky silken cover of your wildly beating heart.
I want you here, where the dawn hesitates with mercy but then
claws at nighttime like a starved vulture, its neck curved in the belly
of the day and a low hum of near-climax building in the back of its
midway time throat, soaring till its pink lips spread with the cry,
victorious—
And there is sunlight.

ACID

I'm sorry
You will have to escort the band a little further
Push it
March the kink
It's your own bed
Tap step on it
Like Madeira on the water
Kick it till it's gone
Pound it till it's red
Match it, lick the flame when you approach her
Sugarcoated bullets where your tongues both end
Scratch it
Then ache for it for years while you are rotting
Acid burns through letters
That you never did send
Lift it
Hard to be en pointe when your lover
Is spreading her legs on another man's bend?
Shame
They're gonna get you if you waver
Keep your core tight,
Keep the laden led

She killed you on the water
Your one surviving daughter
She killed you on the water
And now that you are dead
She'll kill you on the water
Your one surviving daughter
She'll kill you on the water
And next morning she'll be wed

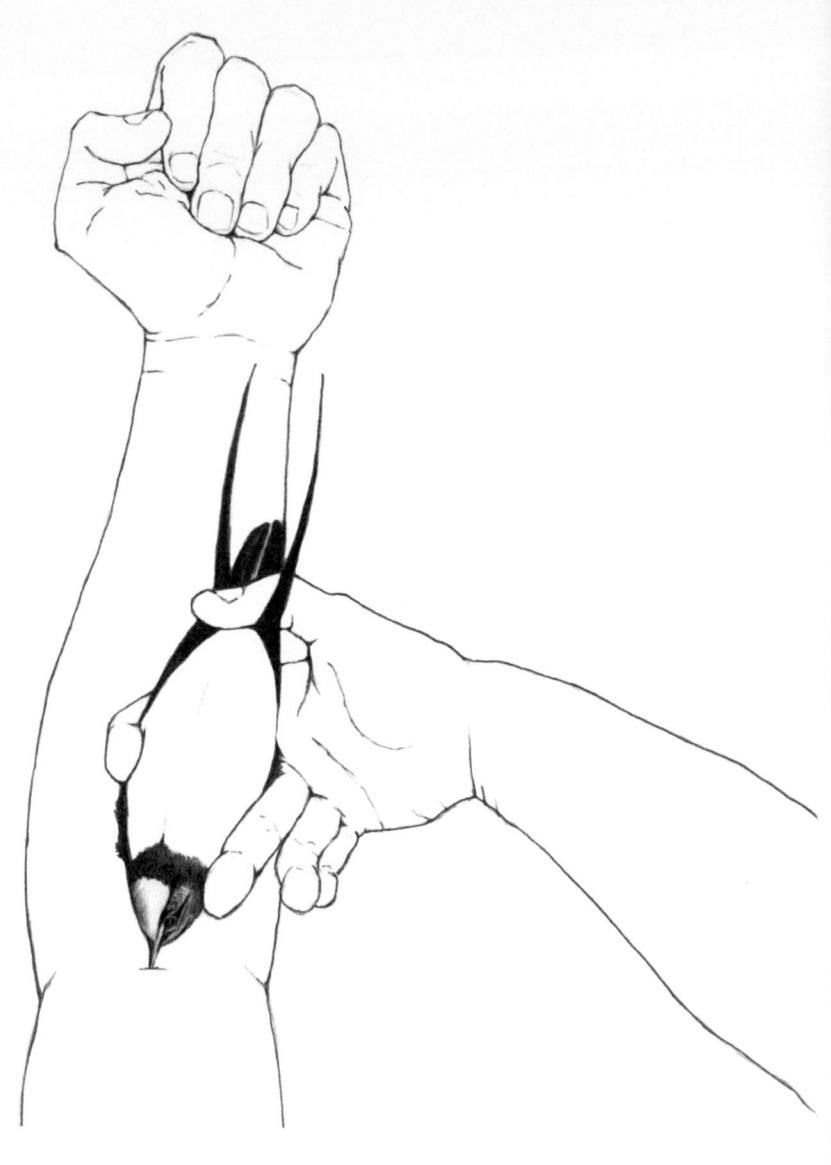

SPEED

When God said for the first time
Let there be light
He didn't mean for the stars to happen
He only meant a small light
And the rest of it to be callous and dry.
It never succeeds no matter how hard I try.
You and I,
Like milking blood to keep,
Syringes to each other's skin,
Is opium poison? Not when it coats
A dagger full of promises
The ratchet weeks pass, and God boasts
I said
Let there be light
And all the stars came to life
I didn't mean for it to be a universal thing
With edges you cannot perceive
I only meant this saccharine speed
To wrap your heart
To make you heave.

TASHLICH

You walk to the riverbank heaven-struck,
Your knuckles slide at your waist,
You delve into the pockets of your garments and turn them inside out.
The fabric is coarse against the nearly translucent surface of your hands.
The water of the river comes and goes at your bare feet,
The ebb and flow of it rises and retreats with your shallow breath,
Quiet, tucked
At the edges of an untold hush, gentle
Gentle, summoning the tangent plains of your lungs to swell,
Lapping at the even measure of your heart.
You shelter your eyes from the sun with your palm,
Your skin is soft,
The silent imprints at the outline of your fingers
Touch with the muted creases at your brow.
You are reminded of saluting,
You remember that you were a soldier,
Your wars return to you, they bite at the rhythm of the water,
The center of your gravity shifts,
Your heels ache.
Who knew you here?
What sacrifices did you make?
At your house a habit is forming,
The windowpanes are warm,

Your lover touches herself.
Her ribs push against the cover of her at the force of the gasp,
Her hair is spilled upon the white slips of the pillows,
Moisture builds at the base of her thighs,
She closes her eyes,
The uncompromising force of the sun penetrates your guarding hand.
You close your eyes as well.
When you open them again you are in the center of your house,
Thick vines rise from the foundation of it and push
Through the wood and cement and the gray-tinted tiles,
They intertwine at the meeting of the walls,
You can smell your lover while your eyes adjust to the new light.
Your lover is on the bed,
She is spreading her legs slowly and deliberately,
Her hand is curled at the juncture of her thighs,
It is moving ceaselessly, seamlessly.
Your eyes, still sun struck, widen and narrow,
You see your lover moving like a wave,
The room has become a dense garden,
Wild and growing at your river-atoned feet.
You undress,
The garments you peeled off your wet skin melt into the growing ground,
Your gaze meets your lover's.
You emit a sound.

It is the first human sound
In the Garden of Eden of the Room.
Feral and unbound the sound curls itself about the bed,
Around your lover,
Your calves are caressed by new grass,
The measure of your heart is untrimmed.
Your chest expands,
The sheets reveal your lover,
You fall or walk onto the bed.
A hitched and constricted breath rushes through your lips,
It traipses the skin of your lover's abdomen,
Her hips kiss at your palms,
She cranes her neck,
You dunk your chin into the conjunction of her pulsating body,
The leafy blanket of the vines hangs over the bed like a canopy.
The air bucks with contractions.
You arch into your lover.
There is a moment of premeditated hesitation
As you press in your mind an attempt at a calculation
Of the multitude lying beside you,
A trembling hand soothes at your forehead,
A body presses at the curve of you,
Your eyes close again.
You mend the flesh
From pieces
With a great exploration.
The sap of the trees at the garden pools at the foot of your bed
And becomes a river.

MICAH THE PROPHET

I found you
Walking barefoot
On the hinges of your wisdom
At Massachusetts Ave:
A clerk,
For all intents and purposes,
Of the apocalypse
That is biting
At the heels
Of us all.
You spoke softly,
Ambling hushed,
Head
Bowed,
At one personification of commerce
Where Bates and Raleigh meet.
You explained that you had no children,
And she saw that you had no shoes.
Your creased hand curled
Disturbed her.
She walked away,
Defiant.
Your dry skin at the cement made a cracking sound
Like a bobby pin falling from the head
Of a gauche dark child
At a ballet recital full of white mothers,
Hitting the floor thundering
Once,
Then
N e v e r a g a i n.

CRUSADING

Small flames light small spaces
Return them to the sun, and they will fade
I am revering in the meadows and
In all the silent places
I am the one returning by their shade

This dust is dust, and it, too,
Is returning
Confessing lust amid this living snow
My city's dead, its only Romeo
An ailing wind that brushes off the fences
They're kissing wild in all their broken tenses—
I have gone I am going I will go

Recall this home; it is complete
That gripping burgundy, the beat
The thrusting of the dripping heat
Our Mecca shines across the street

I told you how I rose to height
One broken scream of godly might
If all I ever do is write
You'll be the day
And I your night.

STARDUST

Rich like candied fruit, the indentation
That comes to shoulders when they've been
Laden with great weight and then,
At once, freed from it;
Things become elevated
Once they've been sunk
For long enough.

How strange:
Like stardust
Crumbling from the sky
With a dim and soundless moan,
Infinitesimal
Saturating lungs and common bones;
What we beat and breathe
Seems not to always be
What we are shown.
In the chill of orchestral snow
Warm and sonless arms
Always wrap around sweet-smelling stone.

MORE OR LESS

Maybe because of the heat,
Everything looks dusty and railed today
Like a healed scratch down the back
Of someone I never knew.
Made with passion,
But embedded in the skin
For good.
You and I were like that
Little archways that never let us rest
And now when I look at your photos,
I think,
What was it
Was it
Just a dream? I can't
Remember a thing you said
Only the taste of your mouth
And the touch of your hands.
The hallway looks suddenly
Like a perfect place for a wake.
We'll put a table there
And there'll be citrus and meat on it
And everyone will talk about
How beautiful and rich and thick it was
And talented and hooked
And no one will mention all the wars
And all the stupid slaps to the face
And apex of our
Conjoined hands.

I told them,
Look,
It was what it was.
And I don't know her anymore
But can you really peel a scratch
Off your skin like that?
Not even with rubbing alcohol,
My love
100% proof won't help you,
Or should I say me
or maybe us
Here
Leaning at bus stops with your goddamn cigarette,
I don't think I've ever
Loved you

More

Or

Less

I SEE YOU LOWERED STILL

I see you lowered still in the corners of my room,
in the pathways of places, in the shaking
murmur of my thighs where you used to
rest so skilfully, all broken hungry and eternal,
ceaselessly on the
hinges of my
lips

I've come to take no notice of the sweet soft silhouettes
your sculpted shoulders make in the nighttime,
where rest
curls like a rainstruck alley cat
in the stoop of the building where I sleep
and the white and pink noise I make for distraction
is swallowed whole by this darkness;
you sit there regal as a studded sheath
to the stuttering sword of dawn.

I want to write you well and sing you distance
but you are ever so defiant
at the arch of my back, insistent
in the corners of my dreams,
on the thick weight of the tissues of my
told
Heart.

After all,

Dust takes for
                    ever
To settle
In the lungs

SHE WON'T TELL ME THE BODY

She won't tell me the body;

I have movements, like a keeled conjunction I have
Movements, they draw scissor marks between
My thighs where you have spoken,
They wake me from my lonely sleep and
Will my ribs to wrap around a pair of fluttering wings,
Sail lost and sunken ships across my breasts,
I have movements.

If only it were friction
That was the measure for creation
We would create great and lovely blue-and-orange things
With the kissing places right above our hearts
Where the sure and pulsating vein of us
Would bulge until it rises to the shape of a whole new heart,
With a body
And a space above.

I have movements, without you, jagged,
Only more gestures to the great attempt of earth for penitence
At every inch of her turning.

SOON WE WILL BECOME A SONG

Soon we will become a song,
and we will be sung by
all the walkers who learned better than us how to walk
and could therefore remain here to play.
Our fingerprints across one another
will soon become a painting
and they will be gazed upon by busy goers
in the sunlight of some idle day,
and our words will be fresh on the tongues of infants who become
shadows across the horizon as it meets the sea longingly at the
change of the day
like we used to do before we faded to become
the language of the now the ever changing.

Soon we will become a song,
and we will no longer be here.
Our former hands will frame hills that will be torn down
to build houses
and our lifetime will blow mercy on their inhabitants.
Our possession will soon weaken its hold and will become
only a slight breeze on the faces of new lovers,
but our cadence will play clear and fierce in the
wind that tilts the trees down with concern,
and our melody will play in the low hum of soft spoken words
in the ears of sleeping children
and the necks of sleeping wives.

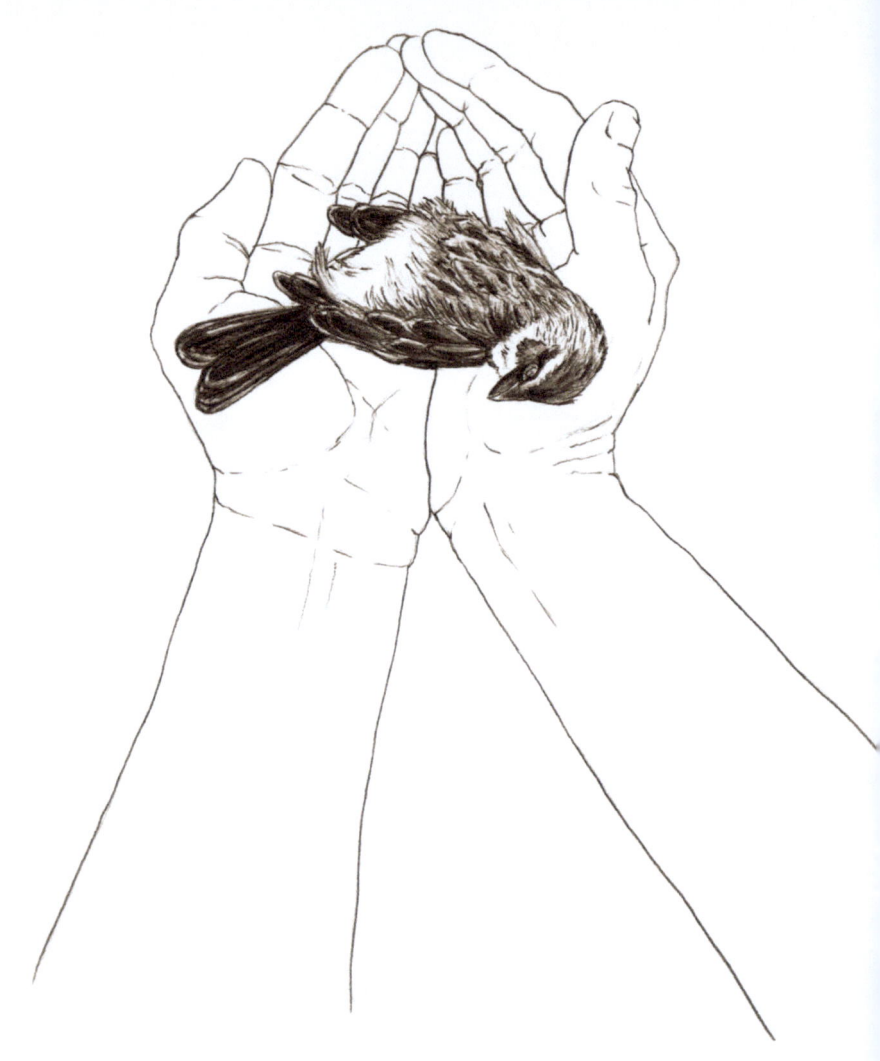

SONG FOR THE BIRD

Once I was a girl
And that was very well
I knew the going of the paths
And I knew the stars that fell.
I knew the morningtime
Atop the mourners' row,
But I was just a girl.
And that was long ago.

Once I was a dove,
And everything was peace
I knew to travel light
I knew that war would cease
I knew to gather water
And how to store it fresh
When I was just a dove
And then they seared my flesh
Now I'm not a girl. Nor am I a dove.

To seek dry shelter
Is all I learned from love.

SONG FOR THE WALKER

Heighten your step
Miserable son
The unending cap
Has brought you undone
Keep at your will
And kneel at the shrine
Walk with the kink
With Venus in trine

Collect at your wrists
The scars that you spoke
Your rain heavy hands
Are ready to soak
The thigh meeting base
That you have left clear
You may no longer wait
For what is left here

At the kick
At the swell
The core
At your throat
Thorough the bounds
You are boat
Row to shore
You can do
Without it
If only
You run

Heighten your step
Miserable son

SONG FOR THE ROAD

My love,
I've held you up for the seven years
My debt
I've bled and wept for it
Returned it for you
A thousand time over

My love,
I've hoped you in the orchards,
With the lilies and in the rain,
I ached you where the roads meet and where my thighs meet
I drew you from the sleep in my eye
I prayed you over the balcony

My love,
The roads that were our roads
I've traveled and traveled over and over again,
I have looked, my love, for traces
In all of the filling places
I have sat in the mouths of whales
And expected in the gardens

My love,
I have retraced and traipsed all the cracks in the wall
Waiting to fill them
Refusing to leave
Even at night
Standing guard over the whole of it

I have, my love
For long enough.
Now that you are well and I am well
I must sing to you distance
And collect the remnants by my own
And gather them in a tower of love
And bend away from it.

Do not be frightened, love.
Do not be alarmed
As to the state
Of my soft muscles.
Do not be sad, my love.
What we had we did have
And in that tower, buried under wreathes of new doings,
There will always be me
And you,
My love.

Here, Now
My token is restored.

Enough.
Enough now.

ACKNOWLEDGMENTS

Providing all I wanted was words, this book is all but it. I want to thank my amazing family, my amazing friends, and all the amazing people who contributed to the journey that is bound here, for you to breathe and take in. It'd be breath wasted to name all the people who helped, literally a song too long to sing and one that would obscure the promise this book holds. I'd like to thank anyone who ever held, inspired, or gifted me with words, who made my body and soul into words, who walked and created words with me. Thank you to the incredible Alex Ogden, without whom my words would be silent and blind.

Gili Estlin Hirsch

I am grateful to all the people I am fortunate enough to know and to have known thus far on my journey for bringing gifts, opportunities, learning experiences, and so much joy into my life.

Mom and Dad, thank you for believing in me, for supporting me, and for loving me no matter what.

Gili Estlin Hirsch, your words make everything possible — all the things. Always.

Alex Ogden

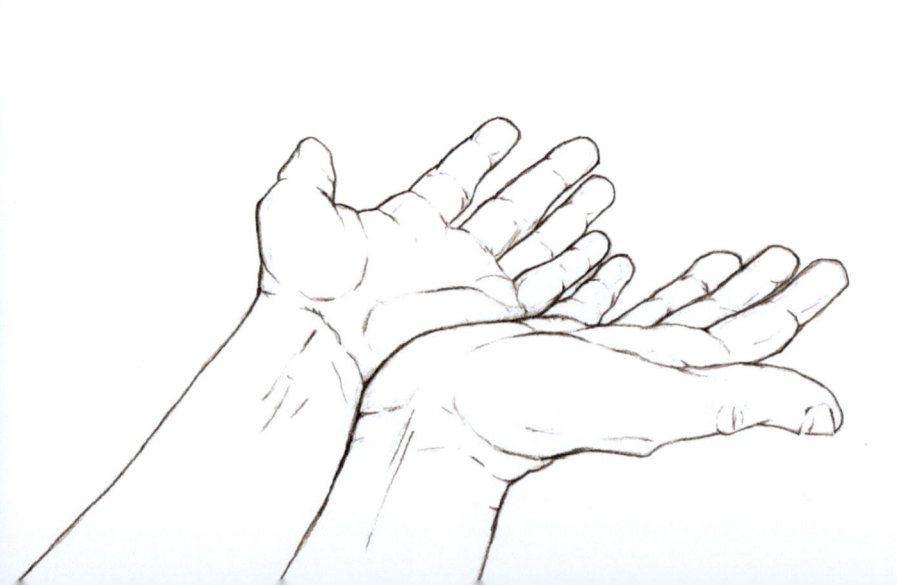

ABOUT THE AUTHOR AND ILLUSTRATOR

GILI ESTLIN HIRSCH is an Israeli-born queer poet who seeks to make words live rather than lie waiting to be read. Gili is the founder of the social poetry movement Apples, Etc. She has been featured in several publications and studied writing in the School of the Arts Institute in Chicago.

www.giliestlinhirsch.com

ALEX OGDEN is a queer visual artist and the owner of Fox & Owl Press. She lives in St. Paul, MN with her two cats.

www.foxandowlpress.com

Printed by Libri Plureos GmbH in Hamburg,
Germany